Simple Acts of Kindness

by
Ray Alonzo

4th Printing

Simple Acts of Kindness
ISBN 1-57757-025-1
Copyright © 1998 by Ray Alonzo
Box 888
Fresno, California 93714-0888

Published by Trade Life Books
P.O. Box 55325
Tulsa, Oklahoma 74155

Introduction

It is so fulfilling to express our love in acts of service to others. There are many occasions that present themselves to us daily, but ordinarily we are too busy or preoccupied to notice them. As a result, we fail to experience the great joy that comes from giving a simple act of kindness.

I have come to see that most of life's joys come from simple interactions that cost little or nothing other than our time and willingness to give. The purpose of this book is to remind us of all the little things we can do to make a big difference in the lives of those we are around and, in turn, those we may never meet. You see, kindness is contagious! It gets under your skin, and once given kindness, it's hard to resist giving it to someone else. So it spreads—hopefully to epidemic proportions.

Pick one thing to do each day. I guarantee if you do, you will find yourself smiling more, loving more, and living life to its fullest. Use this book as a daily reminder that "life is not so much about getting, but more about giving." Who knows, maybe one day you will see the results of your kind act come back around to meet you.

Love your neighbor, as you love yourself.

Dedication

I dedicate this book
to the best mom in the world—Lourdes Alonzo
who taught me the meaning of the word kindness.
I love you Mom.

Simple Acts of Kindness

Little Ways
to Make a
Big Difference

The next time you stay in a hotel,
leave a generous tip in an envelope labeled "maid."

Send a sympathy card to a child who has lost a pet.

Offer to help a student with his homework.

Give your long awaited table at the restaurant
to someone behind you.

Reorganize and clean the silverware drawer.

Give

Buy an inexpensive toy and surprise a neighborhood child.

Give a soft drink to your mechanic.

Write a thank you note to a favorite teacher
from your elementary school years.

Kind

If you are replacing an older car, give it to
a young needy couple instead of selling it.

When washing your own car,
offer to wash your neighbor's car too!

Embrace your spouse often.

Say "thank you" to a referee at the end of a game
(even if your team lost).

Pay for a box of popcorn for the kid behind you
at a movie theater concession.

Collect cans and newspapers for a local charity organization.

Share

Order extra Girl Scout cookies to give to others.

Give your barber or stylist a Christmas gift.

Be courteous to a telemarketer.

Love

Offer to help your neighbor paint his house.

Buy an extra game for the bowlers in the next lane.

Give McDonald's gift certificates to a homeless person.

Care

Pick up trash laying around in your neighborhood.

Start your family's day by making fresh orange juice.

Bake a pie for your neighbor.

Give

Take a couple of casseroles to the home
of a couple with a newborn baby.

Be first to the office and make a pot of coffee.

Send a care package to a college student.

Kind

Join a prison fellowship program.

Give your friends a break by baby-sitting their kids.

Sponsor a child through a relief agency.

Give a candy bar to a tollbooth operator.

Install carbon monoxide and smoke detectors
in your grandparents' house.

Offer to plant some flowers in an elderly person's yard.

Share

Help your neighbor put up their Christmas lights.

Buy your child a one-use camera so they can take
their own pictures on summer vacation.

Buy a gallon of milk and a box of cereal and
stop at a friend's house on a Saturday morning.

Go to a nearby telephone booth and leave
a couple of quarters in the change slot.

Give blood.

Pass out popsicles to the neighbors on a hot Saturday afternoon.

Care

Put a quarter into someone's expired parking meter.

Select an inspirational book to always have on hand
to give to friends and strangers.

Tell your child "I love you" regularly.

Give

Volunteer to help coach a junior sports team.

Surprise your spouse and kids one night by placing
a small chocolate mint on each person's pillow.

Enjoy the sunset with your spouse.

Kind

Post your kid's drawing on the refrigerator.

Play a card or chess game with the seniors at the senior center.

Bring a box of candies for the night shift
at your local rehabilitation center.

Bring fresh-picked flowers to the fire station.

Read an encouraging poem to a cancer patient.

Be the first person to start a conversation.

Share

Offer to buy a postage stamp for a stranger at the post office.

Bring a nice potted plant to work for everyone to enjoy.

Anonymously pay for a full tank of gas for a stranger.

Love

Give the nearby campers your extra firewood.

Bake a batch of cookies for your neighbor.

Send a pizza over to your friend's house (prepaid of course).

Care

Buy lunch for a coworker.

Comfort the surviving family at the funeral.

Give a "Top ten list" to someone close to you
explaining why they are your friend.

Give

Surprise the children's hospital kids with an electric train.

Give up the remote control (Ha Ha!).

Just listen to someone's problem.

Kind

Help a stranger fix a flat tire.

Say grace with your family before a meal.

Plant a tree in your neighborhood.

Write a thank you note to your waiter or waitress
and leave it with your tip.

Take a box of your old toys to the homeless shelter.

Give a fresh flower arrangement to a total stranger.

If you borrow someone's car, return it with a full tank of gas.

When you receive excellent service from someone,
write a note of commendation and give to his or her manager.

Listen to your kids.

Love

Give regular hugs and kisses.

Give a twenty dollar bill to the groom after a wedding ceremony.

Buy pizza for a group of teens who are hanging out.

Care

Bring bagels and cream cheese for the whole office.

Slip a dollar or two in your child's pocket.

Give a friend a facial.

Give

Organize a block party.

Donate old games to a local senior citizen center.

Give your roommate a gift certificate to a discount center.

Kind

Teach your favorite hobby to a child.

Give someone a bag of groceries.

Offer to run an errand for a neighbor.

Thank your spouse regularly.

Kiss your spouse before going to work.

Keep in touch with your teen; buy him or her a pager.

Share

Send your accountant a paper clip holder.

Take a child from a broken home out for a day of fun.

Invite a brother or sister-in-law's kids to a ball game.

Love

Bake a lasagna dinner for your friend's family.

Communicate regularly with your spouse.

Go for a short walk with a friend.

Play catch with the neighborhood kids.

Just be good company and listen to a friend
without interrupting.

House sit for your neighbor.

Give

Call a longtime friend who lives out of town
just to say "hello."

Help a local youth by being a big brother or big sister.

Watch a sunset with a friend.

Kind

Surprise your daughter with a goldfish.

Smile at all times.

Offer your newspaper to someone as you leave
a restaurant.

Call your in-laws and thank them
for raising your spouse as they did.

Bring a small gift to a sick person.

Take your nephew or niece to the local library.

Share

Shovel the snow off your neighbors' driveway
before they leave for work.

When you buy a new coat, take the used one to a homeless shelter.
Don't forget a pair of warm gloves.

Pay the person's toll behind you.

Love

Encourage your spouse regularly.

Wave, smile, and say "hello" to a nearby shopper.

Redeem your aluminum cans and
take the proceeds to a charity organization.

Care

Surprise a friend with a key chain from
his favorite pro sport team.

Bag your garbage tightly for the garbage collector.

Take the whole family to the local zoo for the day.

Give

While at the gas station offer to clean someone's windshield.

Serve your kids breakfast in bed.

Offer to pray for someone who has told you about a problem.

Kind

Bring the whole family to the parade.

Bake blueberry muffins for your neighbors
on a Saturday morning.

Drop your leftover change in the charitable can.

Thank the doorman with a hand shake.

Throw a surprise birthday party for a coworker.

Mow your neighbor's lawn.

Share

Take a small gift when invited to a friend's house.

Always participate in programs like Toys for Tots.

Surprise your spouse with a kiss under some mistletoe.

Love

Share your umbrella with a friend.

Gather a big box of your used clothing and
take it to your local Salvation Army.

Go to your local Red Cross and learn CPR.

Care

Leave a candy bar in the mailbox for your mailman.

Give a child in your neighborhood
a box of crayons.

Volunteer a couple of hours at the soup kitchen.

Give

Delight your son with his favorite poster.

Donate a basketball to your local youth group.

Include a stick of gum when you send birthday cards to children.
(Not a substitute for money!)

Kind

Cook a pot of hearty chicken soup for someone who is sick.

After lunch, offer everyone you work with a mint.

Teach your nephew how to ride a bike.

Write a note of thanks to the local peace officer
who patrols your neighborhood.

Without occasion, send a post card to your grandparents.

Give someone a yo-yo.

Invite your waitress to sit and
visit with you for a few minutes.

Include a stick of gum when you send your utility bills.

Read an adventure book to a kindergarten class.

Forgive and forget.

Give your in-laws framed photos of your family.

Take your wife to a romantic movie.

Give the outdoor toys your children have outgrown,
to a needy family.

Cuddle your son or daughter.

Take a friend bargain shopping.

Give

Buy massage lotion and give your spouse a foot rub.

Sew the buttons on your husband's dress-shirt.

Pay for the person's meal who is
behind you in the drive-through.

Kind

Leave a quarter near the jukebox for someone.

Call your friend and tell her a funny joke.

Car pool with your coworkers.

Thank

Send your mayor a note of appreciation.

Invite a neighbor over for some iced tea.

Make your child laugh; tickle him.

Share

Prepare a home-cooked meal for a college student
who attends your local church.

Keep a supply of stickers to give to kids.

Polish your pregnant wife's toenails.

Love

Watch cartoons with your kids on Saturday.

Clip a great news article for your friend.

Help push a stranger's stalled vehicle
out of the intersection.

Care

Make a quilt for your grandkids.

Send a college friend a prepaid calling card.

Serenade your wife with your guitar.

Give

Buy your son his favorite computer software.

Send a fresh, live lobster to a family member.

Keep an open dish of candy on your desk for coworkers.

Kind

Set up a free lemonade stand.

Donate a teddy bear to a children's hospital.

Yield a convenient parking space to someone else.

Say "thanks" to a security guard where you work.

Take your child on a fishing trip.

Buy grandma or grandpa a walking stick.

Share

Buy a cup of coffee for the Salvation Army bell ringer.

Include your kids when baking cookies.

Give your wife a single long-stemmed red rose.

Love

Surprise your husband with a new pair of boxer shorts.

Donate an ant farm to a kindergarten class.

Let your spouse pick the movie to watch.

Care

Offer to clean your spouse's office.

Send a pack of postage stamps
or stationery to a local prisoner.

Let the people in line who are
in a hurry go ahead of you.

Give

Tell your child a bedtime story.

Take some fresh flowers tied with a ribbon
to a resident at a local nursing home.

Stick an "I Love You" note
in your child's lunch box.

Copy your daughter's or granddaughter's favorite recipes
you fixed for her when she was a child, and
give them to her as a wedding present.

Help type a term paper for a student in your community.

Offer to baby-sit the children in a large family at no charge
so their parents can go on a date.

Send some cookies and a note of thanks
to your child's teacher.

Volunteer to teach a holiday craft to a class
at an elementary school.

Invite an international college student
to your home for a holiday.

Scrape off the ice on your neighbor's windshield.

Offer to spend an evening with an elderly person so
her caregiver may have an evening out.

Volunteer to help with your local Special Olympics competition.

Love

Spend an hour a week teaching something new
to a child with special needs.

Write a letter to someone else's child at camp.

Visit a friend, taking with you
a pint of ice cream and two spoons.

Care

Give five dollars to a friend's child and offer to take him
to buy Christmas presents for his parents.

When purchasing your child's back-to-school supplies,
but an extra set for a needy child.

Surprise a newlywed with a brand new sofa.

Give

Offer to go for a short walk with an elderly neighbor.

Make a plate of goodies for the cafeteria workers
at your child's school.

Compliment your server on
something you like about him or her.

Kind

When you go grocery shopping, buy an extra soda
and a candy bar for your sacker.

Buy a book for a child and offer to read it with him.

Leave a dollar bill on someone's windshield in the parking lot.

Write short notes to your friends thanking them for special qualities you have learned from them.

Volunteer to ring a bell for the Salvation Army at
your local shopping center during the Christmas season.

Call some friends just to let them know you're thinking about them.

Offer to help a friend with a home improvement project.

Help an elderly person address Christmas cards.

Buy some note cards and stamps
for a friend who enjoys writing letters.

Love

Put a nice note in your spouse's lunch.

When you ask people how they are, really listen.

On a holiday, take a plate of goodies to the workers
at a convenience store you frequent.

Write a note of encouragement to a student
you've heard is doing well in school.

Buy craft supplies for a needy family to make
Christmas gifts for their friends and relatives.

Volunteer to go play games with children in a nearby hospital.

Give

Offer to pull weeds from an elderly neighbor's flower bed.

Offer a ride to a person whose car is broken down.

Take a meal to someone who recently lost a loved one.

Kind

Sprinkle bird seed on the window ledge
of someone who is homebound.

Send a note of praise to an outstanding coworker.

Offer to go grocery shopping for an elderly person.

Love your neighbor as yourself.

Note to the Reader

My one great motivation in life is to see a chain reaction of kindness explode around the world—one person at a time.

If this book has inspired you or if you have a few unique ideas to share, I'd love to hear from you!

Ray Alonzo
The Barnabas Group
Box 888
Fresno, CA 93714-0888

Additional copies of this book are
available from your local bookstore.

Trade Life Books
Tulsa, Oklahoma